THE SCIENCE OF

LIGHT

PROJECTS AND EXPERIMENTS
WITH LIGHT AND COLOUR

TABLETOP SCIENTIST – LIGHT
was produced by

David West ☆☆ Children's Books

7 Princeton Court
55 Felsham Road
London SW15 1AZ

Designer: Rob Shone
Editor: Gail Bushnell
Picture Research: Gail Bushnell

First published in Great Britain by Heinemann
Library, Halley Court, Jordan Hill, Oxford
OX2 8EJ, part of Harcourt Education.
Heinemann is a registered trademark
of Harcourt Education Ltd.

09 08 07 06 05
10 9 8 7 6 5 4 3 2 1

ISBN 0 431 01336 5 (HB)
ISBN 0 431 01342 X (PB)

British Library Cataloguing in Publication Data

Parker, Steve
The science of light. - (Tabletop scientist)
1. Light - Juvenile literature
I. Title
535

Printed and bound in China

PHOTO CREDITS :
Abbreviations: t-top, m-middle, b-bottom, r-right,
l-left, c-centre.

Pages 24tl –- BSkyB. 3, 4t, 6tl & tr, 8tl, 14m, 16tl &
tr, 18tl, 20tr, 22–23, 28t & r – Corbis Images. 10m &
r – NASA. 20tl (Phil Ball) – Rex Features Ltd.

Every effort has been made to contact copyright
holders of any material reproduced in this book.
Any omissions will be rectified in subsequent
printings if notice is given to the publishers.

With special thanks to the models: Meshach Burton,
Sam Heming De-Allie, Annabel Garnham, Andrew
Gregson, Hannah Holmes, Molly Rose Ibbett,
Margaux Monfared, Max Monfared, Charlotte
Moore, Beth Shon, Meg Shon, William Slater,
Danielle Smale and Pippa Stannard.

*An explanation of difficult words can be
found in the glossary on page 31.*

THE SCIENCE OF
LIGHT

PROJECTS AND EXPERIMENTS WITH LIGHT AND COLOUR

STEVE PARKER

Heinemann
LIBRARY

CONTENTS

Find out about light
and dark with
simple shadows,...

...mirrors that
reflect light, and...

...lenses that can bend light
and help us to see.

INTRODUCTION

Darkness can be worrying and creepy. We prefer 'lightness' – bright light so we can see. Our sense of sight detects light and enables us to move around safely, pick up things and see their details (like this book), appreciate beautiful colours and patterns, and look out for family and friends. The technology of light lets us do far more. We send information with it, from traffic signals, to millions of flashes every second along fibre-optic cables, carrying computer data. We look into our own bodies with microscopes, peer into deep space with telescopes, and record pictures with cameras. Light is even used to heal, in laser surgery. And light travels faster than anything else in the Universe.

Prepare each project carefully and follow the instructions. Remember: real scientists always put safety first.

HOW IT WORKS

These panels explain the scientific ideas on which each project is based, and the processes that make it work.

TRY IT AND SEE

These panels show further ideas to try, so you can experiment and find out more about light.

WARNING
• Never look directly at the Sun.
• Never shine a bright light, such as a torch beam or laser light, at someone's eyes.

Where you see these symbols:

 Ask an adult to help you.

 Project to be done outdoors.

 Sharp tools may be needed.

 Prepare work surface for a messy project.

LIGHT AND DARK

Lack of light means darkness. The main source of light for our world is the Sun. After it sets we have night.

Light is a type of energy we see with our eyes. It is made of electro-magnetic radiation and travels in a straight path. Light waves cannot pass through wood, metal, rock or similar substances. Darkness is easier to understand. It's not energy, or a substance – it's simply the absence of light.

PROJECT: BUILD A SUNDIAL

As the Sun moves across the sky, ever-changing shadows form where light is blocked.

SUNDIAL

WHAT YOU NEED

- **one large and one small square of thick card**
- **glue**
- **ruler**
- **coloured pens**
- **craft knife**

1

CAREFULLY CUT THE SMALLER SQUARE OF CARD DIAGONALLY. MEASURE ONE OF THE SHORTER SIDES OF THE TRIANGLES.

2

STARTING HALFWAY ALONG ONE EDGE OF THE LARGER SQUARE BASE, MAKE A SLIT AS LONG AS THE TRIANGLE'S SHORTER SIDE.

3

GLUE THE TRIANGLE UPRIGHT INTO THE SLIT, WITH THE TRIANGLE'S RIGHT ANGLE AT THE EDGE OF THE SQUARE BASE.

IN THE SHADE

Light usually travels in straight lines. If an object blocks the Sun's light, then the area behind the object is dark. This area is called a shadow. If we are in the shadow of a large object like a tree, we are 'in the shade'. Before clocks and watches, people used sundials to help tell the time. The upright part which casts the shadow (the triangle in this version) is the gnomon.

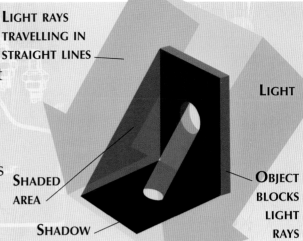

LIGHT RAYS TRAVELLING IN STRAIGHT LINES

LIGHT

SHADED AREA

OBJECT BLOCKS LIGHT RAYS

SHADOW

THE PASSING HOURS

OVER A WHOLE DAY OF SUNSHINE, THE LINES SHOW HOW THE TRIANGLE CASTS A SLOWLY MOVING SHADOW, AS THE SUN PASSES ACROSS THE SKY.

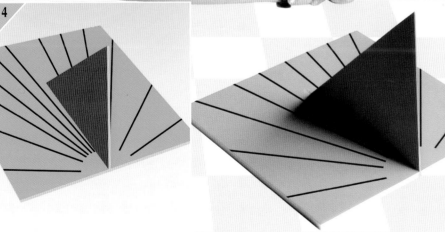

4

IN A SUNNY PLACE, ENSURE THE TRIANGLE'S TALL SIDE POINTS SOUTH. MARK THE SHADOW OF ITS EDGE HOURLY WITH A PEN.

LIGHT SHOW

After a week or so, on another sunny day, put the sundial in the same place. Mark the lines of the shadow again, every hour, with a different coloured pen. Are they in the same place as the previous lines?

FIND OUT HOW THE SUN ALTERS ITS PATH ACROSS THE SKY WITH THE CHANGING SEASONS.

LOOK IN THE MIRROR

Still water's smooth surface reflects light – is this photo upside down?

When light waves hit an object, what happens depends on the surface of the object. If the surface is very smooth, shiny, and flat, like a mirror, the waves bounce off. This bouncing back is reflection. Because of the reflected light, we see an image of the object in the mirror.

PROJECT: BUILD A KALEIDOSCOPE

A submarine's periscope (see opposite) uses mirrors to look above the surface of the water.

KALEIDOSCOPE

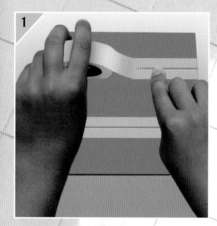

TAPE ALONG THE BACKS OF THE MIRRORS, ON THE LONG SIDES.

WHAT YOU NEED

- **three small mirrors**
- **tracing paper**
- **thin card**
- **strong tape**
- **small beads**
- **coloured paper**
- **torch**

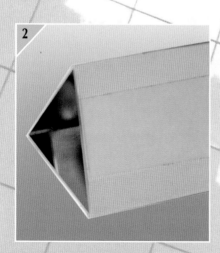

ANGLE THE THREE MIRRORS INTO A TRIANGLE, REFLECTING SURFACES INWARD. TAPE THE TWO REMAINING LONG SIDES.

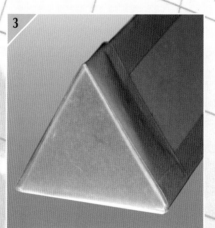

FOLD AND TAPE TRACING PAPER OVER ONE END OF THE KALEIDOSCOPE AND THIN CARD OVER THE OTHER END.

MAKE A SMALL HOLE IN THE MIDDLE OF THE CARD TRIANGLE. DROP THROUGH SMALL BEADS AND BITS OF COLOURED PAPER.

MIRRORS AND ANGLES

Light bounces or reflects off a mirror, at the same angle as it hits. The light waves are called incident when coming to the mirror, and reflected when leaving it. The law of reflection says: angle of incidence = angle of reflection. These angles are measured between the light and an imaginary line, the normal, at right angles (90°) to the mirror. When we look at a mirror, an object which is really in front of it seems to be behind it; what we see is the image.

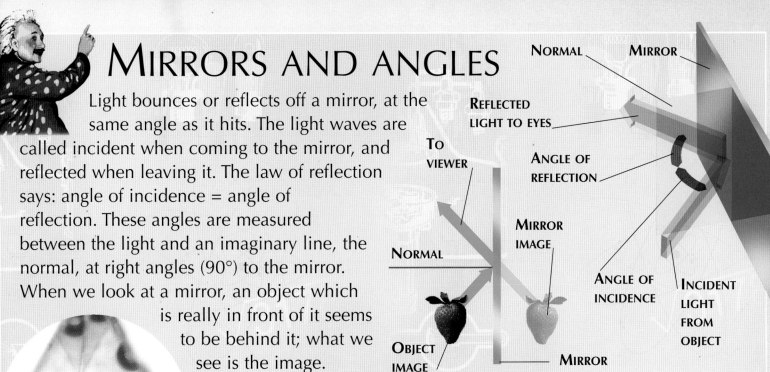

NORMAL   MIRROR
REFLECTED LIGHT TO EYES
TO VIEWER
ANGLE OF REFLECTION
MIRROR IMAGE
NORMAL
ANGLE OF INCIDENCE   INCIDENT LIGHT FROM OBJECT
OBJECT IMAGE
MIRROR

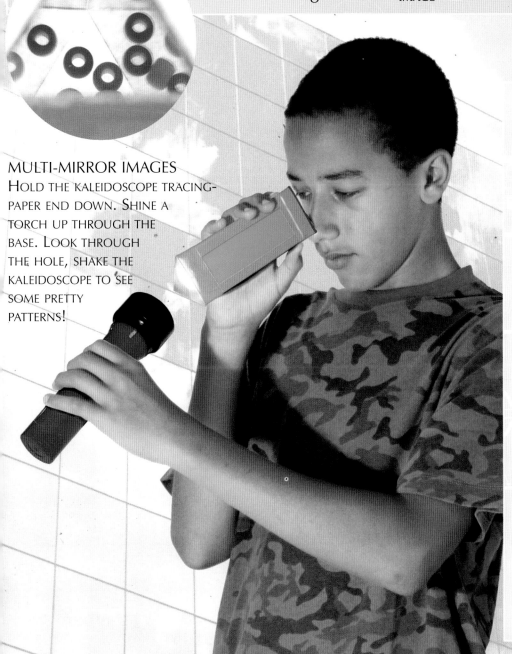

MULTI-MIRROR IMAGES
HOLD THE KALEIDOSCOPE TRACING-PAPER END DOWN. SHINE A TORCH UP THROUGH THE BASE. LOOK THROUGH THE HOLE, SHAKE THE KALEIDOSCOPE TO SEE SOME PRETTY PATTERNS!

IMAGE SHIFT

Try making a periscope using two mirrors, each set at 45° at the end of a long box. For each mirror, the angles of incidence and reflection add up to 90°. So the light comes out of the bottom of the periscope in the same direction as it went in at the top.

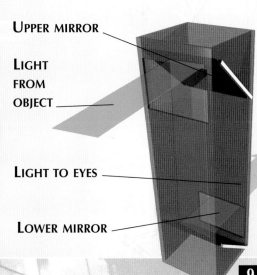

UPPER MIRROR
LIGHT FROM OBJECT
LIGHT TO EYES
LOWER MIRROR

BIGGER AND SMALLER

Mirrors can do strange things. A curved mirror makes the light rays spread out or come together (depending on its shape). This means we see images which are smaller or larger than the original objects.

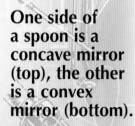

One side of a spoon is a concave mirror (top), the other is a convex mirror (bottom).

The Hubble Space Telescope (HST) has a concave (dished) mirror 2.4 metres across. At the other end its 'door' opens to let in light.

The HST's mirror brings us amazing images of star clouds deep in space.

PROJECT: BUILD A TELESCOPE

WHAT YOU NEED

- **corrugated cardboard**
- **magnifying (make-up or shaving) mirror**
- **flat mirror**
- **magnifying glass**
- **thick card**
- **shoe box**
- **straw**
- **glue**
- **tape**
- **craft knife**

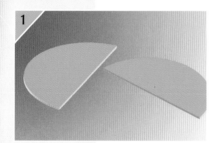

1 TRIM A CARD CIRCLE THE SAME SIZE AS THE MAGNIFYING MIRROR AND CUT THIS CIRCLE IN HALF.

2 GLUE THE HALF-CIRCLES TO A LENGTH OF CORRUGATED CARD, TO MAKE A HALF-TUBE SHAPE.

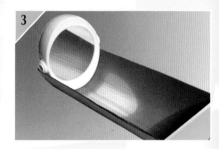

3 TAPE THE MIRROR INTO ONE END OF THE HALF-TUBE, WITH THE MAGNIFYING SIDE INWARDS.

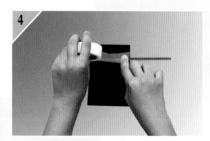

4 TAPE A STRAW TO THE BACK OF A FLAT MIRROR, NEAR ONE OF ITS ENDS. PUT THIS MIRROR IN THE END OF THE HALF-TUBE FACING THE MAGNIFYING ONE.

5 STAND JUST ABOVE AND BEHIND THE MAGNIFYING MIRROR. ALTER THE FLAT MIRROR'S ANGLE UNTIL YOU CAN SEE THE MAGNIFYING MIRROR IN IT.

6 CUT HALF-CIRCLES AT THE TWO ENDS OF A SHOE BOX, EACH WIDE ENOUGH FOR THE HALF-TUBE. TAPE THE HALF-TUBE AND ITS MIRRORS INTO THIS BASE.

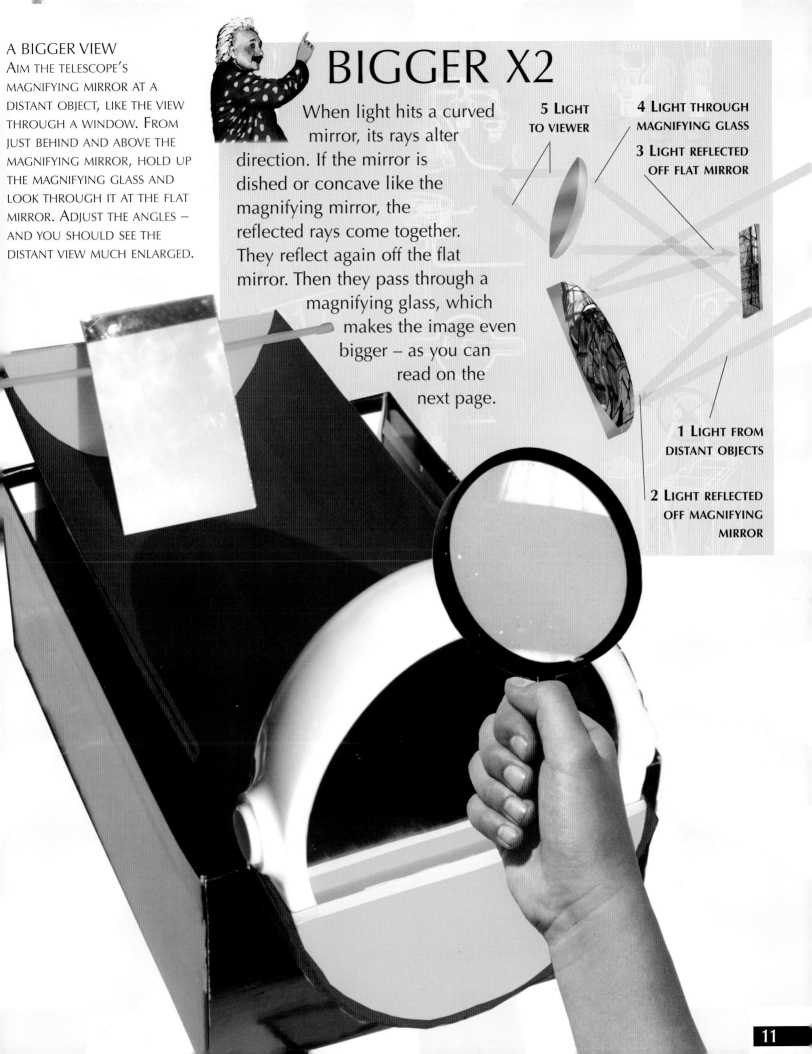

A BIGGER VIEW

Aim the telescope's magnifying mirror at a distant object, like the view through a window. From just behind and above the magnifying mirror, hold up the magnifying glass and look through it at the flat mirror. Adjust the angles — and you should see the distant view much enlarged.

BIGGER X2

When light hits a curved mirror, its rays alter direction. If the mirror is dished or concave like the magnifying mirror, the reflected rays come together. They reflect again off the flat mirror. Then they pass through a magnifying glass, which makes the image even bigger – as you can read on the next page.

5 Light to viewer

4 Light through magnifying glass

3 Light reflected off flat mirror

1 Light from distant objects

2 Light reflected off magnifying mirror

WHEN LIGHT BENDS

Light goes in a straight line, unless something gets in the way. Substances like air, water, and glass are transparent, meaning light passes through them. The light still travels in a straight line but it changes direction when it hits a new substance.

PROJECT: A LENS JAR

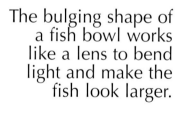

The bulging shape of a fish bowl works like a lens to bend light and make the fish look larger.

LENS JAR

MAKE TWO SLITS ABOUT 5 CM LONG AND 2 CM APART IN ONE END OF THE CARDBOARD BOX.

WHAT YOU NEED

- **cardboard box**
- **sheet of white paper**
- **glass jar**
- **water**
- **torch**
- **scissors**

COVER THE BOX'S BASE WITH WHITE PAPER. PUT A JAR OF WATER ON THIS, IN THE MIDDLE OF THE BOX.

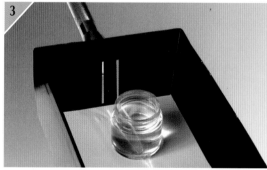

IN DARK CONDITIONS, SHINE A TORCH THROUGH THE SLITS INTO THE BOX, AIMING AT THE JAR.

REFRACTION

The bending of light as it passes from one transparent substance to another, like air to water, or water to glass, is called refraction. A curved transparent object, known as a lens, refracts light in a certain way. The version shown here is a bulging or convex lens (wider in the middle than around the edges). It makes the light beams come together, or converge. Find out how lenses can be used on the next page.

GLASS

LIGHT

FIRST REFRACTION

WATER

SECOND REFRACTION

DOUBLE BEAM
THE SLITS LET THROUGH TWO NARROW BEAMS OF LIGHT. AS THESE HIT THE JAR, THEY BEND INWARDS. THEY DO THE SAME AS THEY LEAVE THE JAR, BENDING IN OR CONVERGING. THE PLACE WHERE THE BEAMS CROSS IS CALLED THE FOCAL POINT.

SEEING DOUBLE

Put a coin in a tumbler part-filled with water. Adjust your view – and see two coins! Some light passes from the coin through the water and side of the tumbler to your eyes. Other beams pass up to the surface of the water and then bend or refract into the air, and through the side to your eyes.

VIEW THROUGH WATER'S SURFACE

VIEW THROUGH WATER AND GLASS

ALL ABOUT LENSES

Lenses are used in telescopes, magnifiers, binoculars, and cameras – and inside us, too. Each of our eyes has a convex lens (one that bulges in the middle, see page 22). Through this we see the world. In general, convex lenses magnify, making things look bigger. The other main type of lens is concave (thinner in the middle than around the edges). It makes items look smaller.

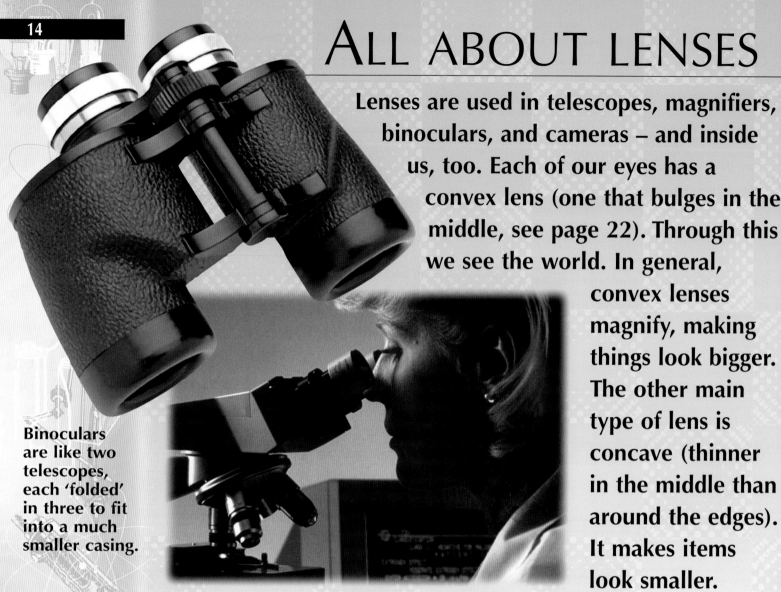

Binoculars are like two telescopes, each 'folded' in three to fit into a much smaller casing.

A binocular microscope has two eyepiece lenses, one for each eye, and a choice of lenses for different magnifications, usually up to x 100.

PROJECT: BUILD A MICROSCOPE

MICROSCOPE

WHAT YOU NEED

- **small plastic bottle**
- **stiff clear plastic**
- **magnifying glass**
- **small paintbrush**
- **scissors**

CUT A SMALL PLASTIC BOTTLE IN HALF. IN THE UPPER (CUT) EDGE OF THE BOTTOM PART, CUT TWO SHALLOW NOTCHES OPPOSITE EACH OTHER.

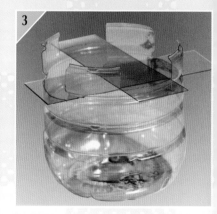

CUT TWO MORE NOTCHES, DEEPER THAN THE FIRST PAIR, OPPOSITE EACH OTHER AND AT RIGHT ANGLES TO THE FIRST TWO NOTCHES.

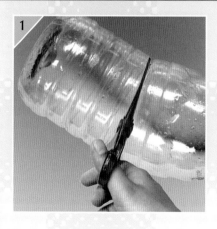

TRIM TWO LONG NARROW STRIPS OF THE CLEAR PLASTIC TO FIT LIKE SHELVES IN THE NOTCHES AND ACROSS THE BOTTLE, ONE SHELF ABOVE THE OTHER.

NEAR...

Light from the object (specimen) passes through the first, or objective, lens. It bends inwards, or converges (see page 13). When you look through, you see an enlarged image. The magnifier near your eye is the second, or eyepiece, lens. Also convex, it works as a second enlarger to make the view through the objective lens even bigger.

CONVEX LENS (DROP)

LIGHT TO EYE

IMAGE (ENLARGED BY DROP OF WATER)

LIGHT BENT BY LENS

OBJECT (ACTUAL SIZE)

EYEPIECE LENS (MAGNIFYING GLASS)

LIGHT

OBJECTIVE LENS (WATER DROP)

OBJECT (SPECIMEN)

Light from the object (specimen) passes through the first, or objective, lens. It bends inwards, or converges (see page 13).

MINI TO MAXI

BRING YOUR EYE VERY CLOSE TO THE WATER DROP. ITS CURVED SURFACE ACTS AS A CONVEX LENS TO MAGNIFY THE SPECIMEN, HERE A FLY. NOW HOLD THE MAGNIFYING GLASS ABOVE THE DROP AND LOOK THROUGH IT. MOVE IT UP AND DOWN TO BRING AN EVEN MORE ENLARGED VIEW INTO FOCUS.

4

PLACE A SMALL ITEM TO STUDY, THE SPECIMEN, ON THE MIDDLE OF THE LOWER SHELF. DAB A DROP OF WATER DIRECTLY ABOVE IT, ON THE UPPER SHELF.

...AND FAR

A simple telescope has two lenses, like the microscope. But its objective lens is less curved. It converges light to a point, or focus, farther from the lens. This makes it suitable for looking at very distant objects like stars. The image at the focus is enlarged by the last lens.

TRY TO IDENTIFY THE FOCUS OF THE OBJECTIVE LENS IN THE MICROSCOPE DIAGRAM ABOVE.

EYEPIECE LENS

FOCUS OF OBJECTIVE LENS

ADJUSTABLE SLIDING TUBE

OBJECTIVE LENS

COLOURS OF LIGHT

How many different colours are there? Seven? Fifty? In fact, there are too many to count. Different colours are light waves which have different wavelengths. The longest wavelengths are red light. The shortest wavelengths are violet light. These are the two ends of the range of colours, known as the visible spectrum.

The seven 'rainbow colours' are red, orange, yellow, green, blue, indigo, and violet.

As clear plastic bends its thickness changes slightly. It lets through only some wavelengths of light waves, showing different colours.

PROJECT: MAKE A NO-RAIN RAINBOW

NO-RAIN RAINBOW

WHAT YOU NEED

- **torch**
- **small mirror**
- **shoe box**
- **tape**
- **white card**
- **black card**
- **strip of thick card**
- **small bowl**
- **water**
- **craft knife**

1

PUT THE BOWL, HALF-FILLED WITH WATER, IN THE SHOE BOX. PLACE THE CARD STRIP ACROSS THE TOP AND LEAN THE MIRROR AT AN ANGLE AGAINST IT.

2

TAPE THE WHITE CARD INSIDE ONE END OF THE SHOE BOX, FACING THE MIRROR. CUT A SLIT IN THE BLACK CARD AND TAPE IT OUTSIDE THE SAME END.

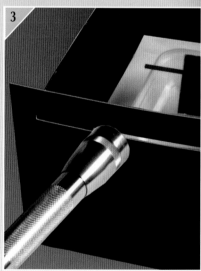

3

THE SLIT SHOULD BE HORIZONTAL, JUST ABOVE THE TOP OF THE WHITE CARD. SHINE THE TORCH THROUGH THE SLIT ON TO THE MIRROR.

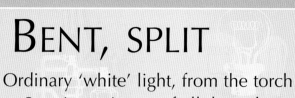

BENT, SPLIT

Ordinary 'white' light, from the torch or Sun, is a mixture of all the colours of light. When the light waves hit the curved edge of the water, the meniscus, they are split or refracted into different colours. The light waves are reflected off the mirror and are refracted again as they leave the water. In a real rainbow, the curved raindrops work like the meniscus and the back of the raindrop works like the mirror.

NARROW TORCH BEAM OF WHITE LIGHT

CURVE OF MENISCUS

RAINBOW

MIRROR

SURFACE OF WATER

WATER

RAINBOW WITHOUT RAIN!

WHEN THE ANGLES OF THE TORCH AND MIRROR ARE RIGHT, A RAINBOW APPEARS ON THE WHITE CARD! RIPPLE THE WATER – DOES THE RAINBOW MOVE? USE YOUR HAND TO BLOCK THE LIGHT AT VARIOUS PLACES. HOW IS THE RAINBOW FORMED?

4

DIM THE LIGHTS IN THE ROOM. ADJUST THE ANGLE OF THE MIRROR BY MOVING THE CARD STRIP TO OR FRO. KEEP LOOKING AT THE WHITE CARD.

BACK TO WHITE

A colour wheel has seven colours of the visible spectrum. When the wheel spins fast, its colours merge or combine – and become white. This is the opposite process to forming a rainbow.

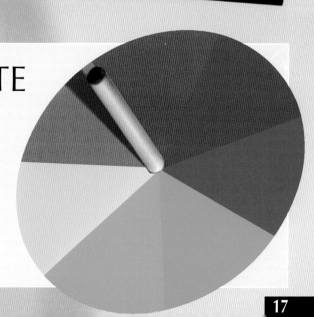

MIX-AND-MATCH COLOURS

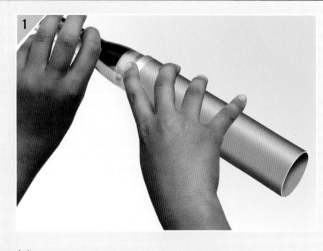

The tiny dots on a TV screen are blue, green, and red. In different combinations they make all other colours.

Ordinary white light is a mixture of all the colours of the spectrum. But you don't really need all these colours, you just need red, green, and blue. They are the primary colours used when light rays are being added together. Mix them in various ways and they make all other colours. Add all three and they make white. You see this daily on TV and computer screens.

PROJECT: ADDING COLOURS

Each piece of the stained glass window lets through only part of white light's colours.

ADDING COLOURS

WHAT YOU NEED

- **three bright torches**
- **printable film**
- **tape**
- **cardboard**

1 MAKE THREE CARDBOARD TUBES AND TAPE ONE TO THE END OF EACH TORCH. PRINT RED, BLUE, AND GREEN SQUARES ON TO A SHEET OF PRINTABLE FILM, USING A COMPUTER.

2 CUT OUT THE COLOURED SQUARES AND ATTACH ONE TO THE END OF EACH TORCH AS A FILTER. IN DARK CONDITIONS, SHINE THE THREE TORCHES AT THE FLOOR SO THAT THEY OVERLAP.

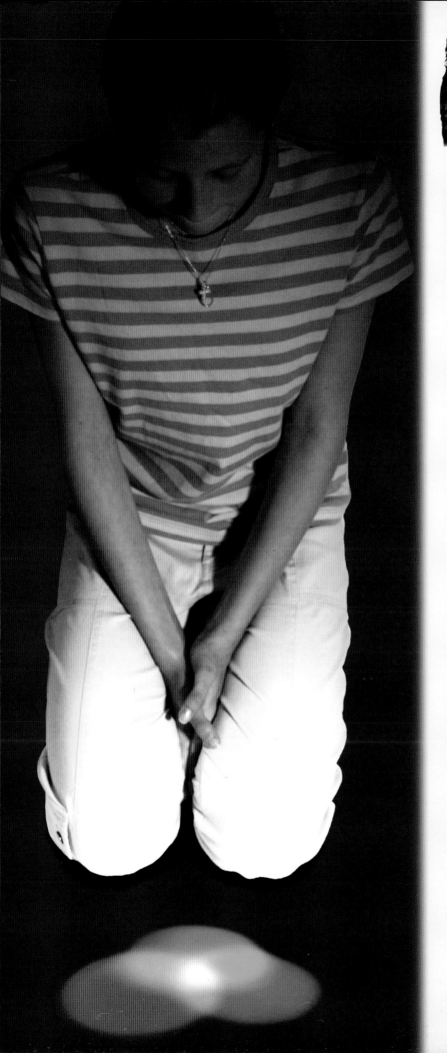

+ AND –

The primary colours of light add up, as shown here. However, if you look at an object which does not make its own light, but reflects it, colours work differently. They do not add up, they take away. A yellow toy car is yellow because when white light hits it, the surface of the car soaks up or absorbs all colours except yellow. With all the other colours taken away, only yellow light is left to travel to your eyes. Dyes, inks, and pigments work in the same take-away way (see next page).

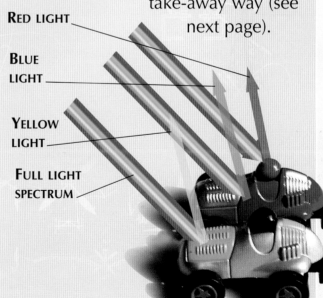

RED LIGHT

BLUE LIGHT

YELLOW LIGHT

FULL LIGHT SPECTRUM

PRIMARY AND SECONDARY

EACH FILTER LETS THROUGH ONLY ONE COLOUR OF LIGHT. ALL THREE PRIMARY COLOURS ADD UP TO MAKE WHITE. THEY ADD UP IN PAIRS TOO, TO MAKE LIGHT'S SECONDARY COLOURS. RED + GREEN = YELLOW, RED + BLUE = MAGENTA, AND GREEN + BLUE = CYAN.

PAINT WITH LIGHT

The pictures on this page may seem to have lots of colours. But look closer and there are only three. These are primary pigments: cyan, yellow, and magenta. Pigments give the colours of inks, paints, dyes, and stains.

An enlarged view shows dots of three primary pigments.

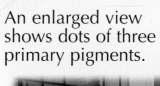

Coloured cloth has taken up complex patterns of many pigments.

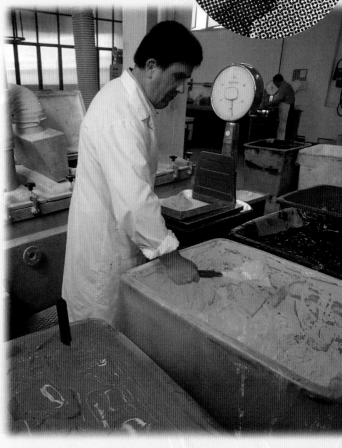

PROJECT: MAKE A COLOUR SPLITTER

Tiny dots of the three primary pigments, in different combinations, make up all other colours in printed pictures like this photo.

WHAT YOU NEED

- **blotting paper**
- **coloured felt-tip pens**
- **paper clips**
- **glass jars**
- **cocktail sticks**
- **scissors**

1

POUR A LITTLE WATER INTO EACH JAR. CUT THE BLOTTING PAPER INTO NARROW STRIPS.

2

USING COLOURED, WATER-BASED FELT-TIP PENS, PUT ONE BLOB OF INK AT ONE END OF EACH STRIP.

3

HANG EACH STRIP FROM A STICK, SO THE BLOBBED END OF THE STRIP JUST TOUCHES THE WATER.

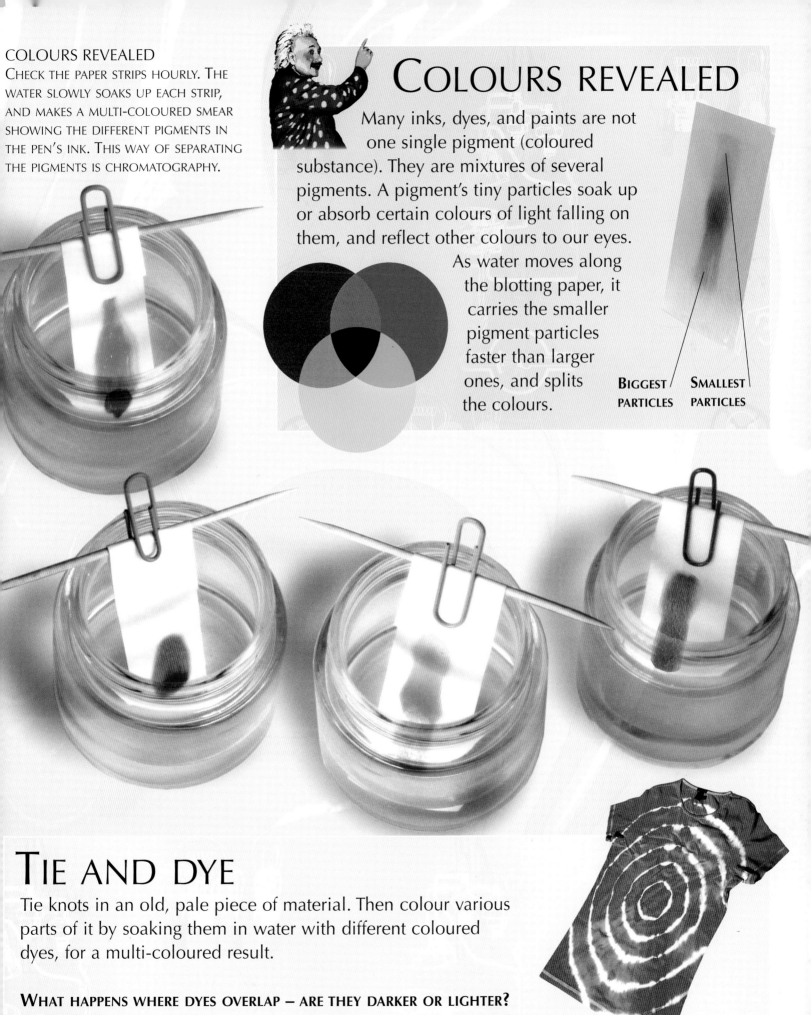

COLOURS REVEALED

CHECK THE PAPER STRIPS HOURLY. THE WATER SLOWLY SOAKS UP EACH STRIP, AND MAKES A MULTI-COLOURED SMEAR SHOWING THE DIFFERENT PIGMENTS IN THE PEN'S INK. THIS WAY OF SEPARATING THE PIGMENTS IS CHROMATOGRAPHY.

COLOURS REVEALED

Many inks, dyes, and paints are not one single pigment (coloured substance). They are mixtures of several pigments. A pigment's tiny particles soak up or absorb certain colours of light falling on them, and reflect other colours to our eyes.

As water moves along the blotting paper, it carries the smaller pigment particles faster than larger ones, and splits the colours.

BIGGEST PARTICLES **SMALLEST PARTICLES**

TIE AND DYE

Tie knots in an old, pale piece of material. Then colour various parts of it by soaking them in water with different coloured dyes, for a multi-coloured result.

WHAT HAPPENS WHERE DYES OVERLAP – ARE THEY DARKER OR LIGHTER?

SEEING LIGHT

For most people, sight is the most important of our five main senses. Our eyes are incredible. Light passes through the clear, outer covering of the eye, the cornea. It is then focused by the lens of the eye to form a clear, sharp image on the back of the eyeball, called the retina. The retina detects different light colours and sends nerve messages to the brain.

The eye's bulging front is the cornea. The coloured part, or iris, adjusts the hole in its centre, the pupil, for dim or bright light.

PROJECT: BUILD
A PINHOLE CAMERA

PINHOLE CAMERA

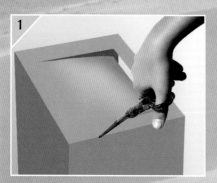

1 CUT A SQUARE HOLE IN ONE END OF EACH BOX.

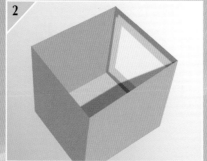

2 ON ONE BOX, TAPE TRACING PAPER OVER THE SQUARE HOLE.

WHAT YOU NEED

- two small cardboard boxes
- sheet of tracing paper
- tape
- scissors
- pin

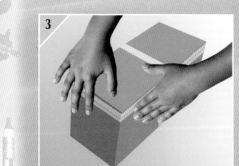

3 TAPE THE BOXES TOGETHER SO THE SQUARE HOLE OF ONE IS AGAINST THE TRACING PAPER OF THE OTHER. TAPE THE LIDS TOO.

4 AT ONE END OF THE DOUBLE-BOX, MAKE A TINY HOLE OR PINHOLE 1–2 MM ACROSS, IN THE CENTRE.

5 IN THE DOUBLE-BOX'S OTHER END, MAKE AN EYEHOLE 15 MM ACROSS. TAPE OVER ALL OTHER GAPS FOR A DARK INTERIOR.

EYE AND CAMERA

Cameras and eyes focus light to form an image on a surface – the eye's retina and the pinhole camera's tracing paper. This camera does not have an adjustable lens, like the eye. It relies on light coming through a tiny hole. The way the light rays cross over means that the image is upside down in both the eye and the camera. However, when we are babies, the brain soon learns to turn the image from the eye the right way up.

OBJECT

LIGHT TO CAMERA

PINHOLE 'LENS'

IMAGE ON TRACING PAPER

NERVE TO BRAIN

LENS

CORNEA

OBJECT

IMAGE ON RETINA

PUPIL

IRIS

LIGHT TO EYE

SEE THE SCENE
POINT THE PINHOLE CAMERA AT A BRIGHT SCENE, SUCH AS THROUGH A WINDOW. LOOK INTO THE EYEHOLE – AND YOU CAN SEE THE SCENE ON THE TRACING PAPER. BUT THERE'S SOMETHING STRANGE – IT'S UPSIDE DOWN!

FOOL EYE OR BRAIN?

The eye simply records a scene and sends messages to the brain. But the brain may have trouble working out what some scenes mean.

STARE AT ONE OF THESE WHITE DOTS. DO THE DOTS AROUND IT LOOK DARKER? LOOK AT ONE OF THEM – DOES IT TURN WHITE?

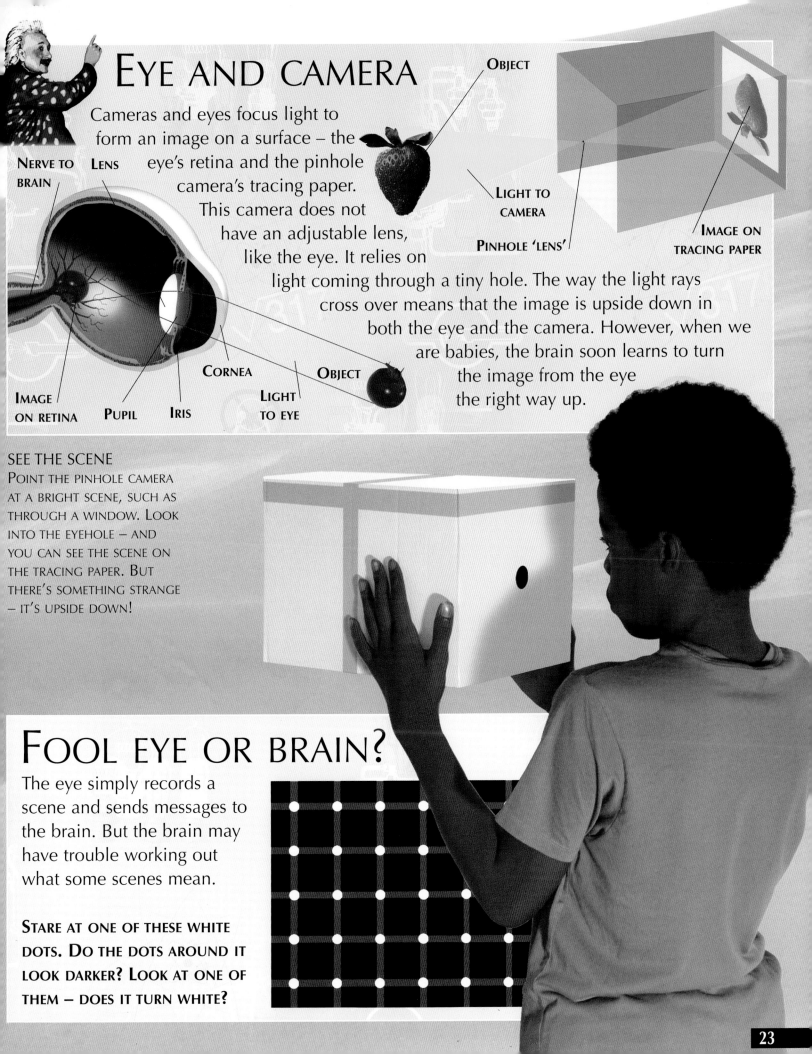

MOVING IMAGES

'Live' TV cameras send their still pictures directly to the studio.

As you watch action on television, like people running – they aren't. You see still pictures that follow each other rapidly, many each second. This is too quick for the eye to see separately so they blur into motion.

Movie cameras record 24 pictures per second on a long reel of film.

PROJECT: BUILD A PRAXINOSCOPE

PRAXINOSCOPE

WHAT YOU NEED

- **black card**
- **dinner plate**
- **white paper**
- **pencil**
- **ruler**
- **small nail**
- **mirror**
- **bead**
- **cork**
- **glue**
- **craft knife**
- **scissors**

1

GLUE THE WHITE PAPER TO THE BLACK CARD. DRAW AROUND THE PLATE ON THEM. CUT OUT A DISC.

DRAW A DESIGN LIKE THE ONE PICTURED HERE, SHOWING A MOVEMENT IN 12 SEPARATE STAGES. MAKE THE DIFFERENCE BETWEEN ONE STAGE AND THE NEXT QUITE SMALL. CUT OUT THE 12 DRAWINGS. GLUE EACH TO THE WHITE SIDE OF THE DISC, ON ONE OF THE LINES DRAWN IN STEP 2. POSITION EACH DRAWING MIDWAY BETWEEN THE OUTER END OF THE VIEWING SLIT AND THE DISC'S EDGE.

2

DRAW 12 EQUALLY SPACED LINES (30° APART) FROM THE DISC'S CENTRE TO ITS EDGE.

4

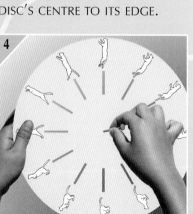

CAREFULLY PUSH A SMALL NAIL THROUGH THE DISC'S CENTRE, FROM THE WHITE SIDE.

3

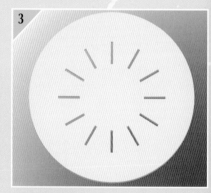

CUT A SLIT ON EACH LINE, ONE-QUARTER OF THE WAY FROM THE CENTRE TO HALFWAY ALONG.

5

ON THE BLACK SIDE, SLIP A BEAD OVER THE NAIL. PUSH THE NAIL'S POINT INTO THE CORK.

TOO FAST TO SEE

As the disc spins, you see through each slit for a fraction of a second. When the next slit comes around, you get another split-second view of the drawings, and so on. This happens so fast, the eye merges the separate drawings to give an impression of movement. A movie camera works in a similar way, taking many still pictures or 'frames' each second (right).

1 ROTATING SHUTTER CUTS OFF LIGHT TO FILM STRIP
2 CLAW PULLS FILM STRIP ALONG BY ONE FRAME
3 CLAW WITHDRAWS, SHUTTER CONTINUES TO TURN
4 LIGHT PASSES THROUGH 'GATE' (HOLE) TO MAKE STILL IMAGE OR FRAME ON FILM

ROTATING SHUTTER
GATE
CLAW

SPINNING INTO ACTION

YOU HAVE MADE AN OLD-FASHIONED TOY CALLED A PRAXINOSCOPE. STAND IN FRONT OF A MIRROR. HOLD UP THE DISC SO YOU CAN PEER FROM THE BLACK SIDE THROUGH THE TOPMOST SLIT. LOOK STEADILY AT THE REFLECTION OF THE WHITE SIDE IN THE MIRROR — AND SPIN THE DISC. SEE HOW THE DRAWINGS 'LEAP INTO LIFE' AND APPEAR TO MOVE.

HOW SLOW?

Spin the disc at different speeds. Too fast and your eyes do not have time to register the pictures, too slow and the motion becomes jerky.

TRY TO WORK OUT THE SPEED, IN FRAMES PER SECOND, WHEN YOU SEE THE PICTURES AS SEPARATE DRAWINGS.

RODS OF LIGHT

An optical engineer (a scientist specializing in light) tests a laser in the laboratory.

Light travels in straight lines and can be made to turn corners. But it always travels along a straight path, or a few straight paths. An optical fibre is a bendy rod of clear plastic or glass. Light within the rod reflects off the inside of its surface and zig-zags along, even around bends. Optical fibres often carry laser light.

PROJECT: BUILD A LIGHT ROD

Fibre-optic bundles are put together into optical cables.

LIGHT ROD

WHAT YOU NEED

- **plastic bottle**
- **black paint**
- **torch**
- **pin**
- **modelling clay**
- **shallow bowl**

1. CUT THE TOP OFF THE PLASTIC BOTTLE. PAINT IT BLACK ON THE OUTSIDE. MAKE A NEAT HOLE NEAR ITS BASE WITH THE PIN.

2. ON THE SIDE DIRECTLY OPPOSITE THE PINHOLE, SCRAPE A SMALL PATCH OF PAINT FROM THE BOTTLE TO REVEAL THE PLASTIC.

3. COVER THE PINHOLE WITH MODELLING CLAY TO SEAL IT. PUT THE BOTTLE IN A SHALLOW BOWL AND FILL IT WITH WATER.

LIQUID LIGHT

Light hits the inside of an optical fibre at such a shallow angle, it reflects back rather than passing through to the outside. Laser light is most useful for this purpose. Unlike ordinary light, its waves are all parallel to each other, and the same length, with their peaks all lined up. Waves of the same length mean that laser light is a single pure colour.

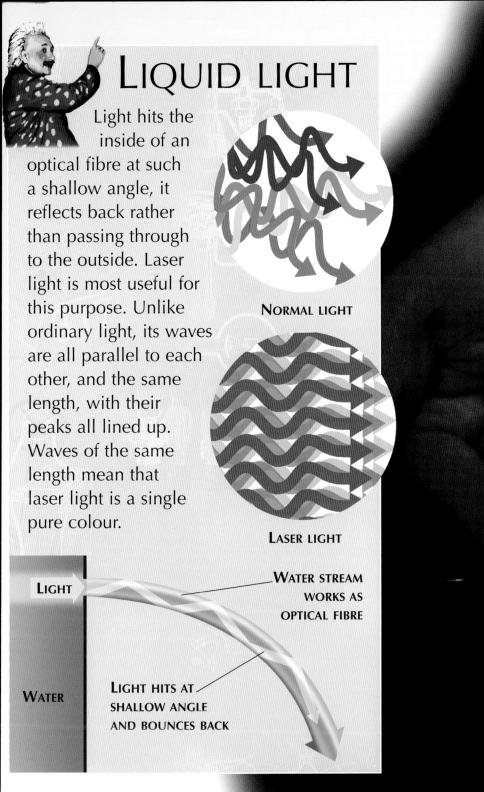

NORMAL LIGHT

LASER LIGHT

LIGHT

WATER

WATER STREAM WORKS AS OPTICAL FIBRE

LIGHT HITS AT SHALLOW ANGLE AND BOUNCES BACK

IN A FLASH

Light flashing on and off can carry information in the form of code. Millions of laser flashes each second travel hundreds of kilometres along optical cables.

TRY TURNING THE TORCH ON AND OFF QUICKLY. HOW FAST CAN YOU SEND A SIMPLE MESSAGE IN MORSE CODE?

BRIGHT SPOT
SHINE A TORCH AT THE AREA OF BLACK SCRATCHED OFF THE BOTTLE. REMOVE THE MODELLING CLAY AND WATCH. WATER PRESSURE MAKES A THIN 'ROD' OF WATER SPURT OUT OF THE SMALL HOLE. SEE HOW IT CARRIES THE TORCH LIGHT AND MAKES A BRIGHT SPOT ON YOUR FINGER.

THE POWER OF LIGHT

Plants are like living chemical factories, with light as the driving power. They provide us and animals with this energy, when we eat them.

Solar power is light energy from the Sun. It is turned directly into electricity by rows of photovoltaic cells.

Light is a form of energy – and one form of energy can change into another. Your eyes make light rays into nerve messages. Plants change light energy into sugary substances they need to live and grow. Solar panels make light into electricity.

PROJECT: MAKE AN AMAZING BEAN MAZE

BEAN MAZE

WHAT YOU NEED

- cardboard box with lid
- bean seed
- small pot of wet soil
- water
- thin black card
- tape
- scissors

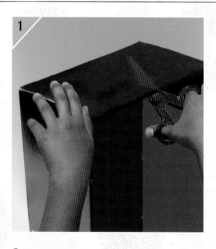

1 SOAK THE BEAN OVERNIGHT IN WATER. PLANT IT IN THE POT OF DAMP SOIL. TAKE OFF OR OPEN THE BOX LID. CUT A SQUARE HOLE AT ONE END OF THE BOX'S NARROWEST, SHORTEST SIDE.

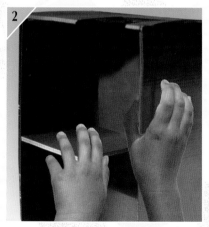

2 CUT TWO LENGTHS OF CARD AS DEEP AS THE BOX BUT NOT AS WIDE. WITH THE HOLE AT THE TOP RIGHT, TAPE THEM INTO THE BOX, ONE TO THE LOWER LEFT AND ONE AT THE UPPER RIGHT.

3 PLACE THE BEAN POT ON THE LOWER LEFT OF THE BOX'S BASE. REPLACE THE BOX LID. PUT THE BOX IN A SUNNY PLACE. WATER THE SOIL EVERY TWO OR THREE DAYS TO KEEP IT DAMP.

LIGHT WORK

Plants use tiny parts known as chloroplasts, which are inside microscopic leaf cells, to catch light energy. The energy is used to combine carbon dioxide gas, taken in from the air, with water, soaked up from the soil. The results are energy-rich sugars, which pass to all parts of the plant, and oxygen, which is released into the air.

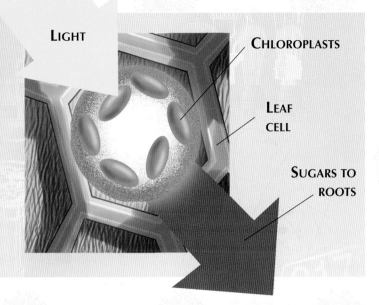

LIGHT

CHLOROPLASTS

LEAF CELL

SUGARS TO ROOTS

STRETCHING TO THE LIGHT

THE BEAN SEED SPROUTS, AND ITS SHOOT STARTS TO LENGTHEN. PLANTS NATURALLY GROW TOWARDS LIGHT SINCE THEY NEED IT TO SURVIVE. THE BEAN SHOOT CAN DETECT LIGHT COMING DOWN FROM THE HOLE, SO IT TWISTS AND TURNS THROUGH THE MAZE TO REACH IT. A-MAZE-ING!

CRESS CROSS

Try planting cress seeds in a shallow tray of soil. Cover them with a card which has a cut-out pattern, like a cross or your initials. Keep the soil moist.

SEE WHAT HAPPENS TO THE SEEDLINGS. THOSE UNDER THE CUT-OUT RECEIVE ENOUGH LIGHT TO GROW WELL. THOSE IN THE DARKER PARTS DO NOT.

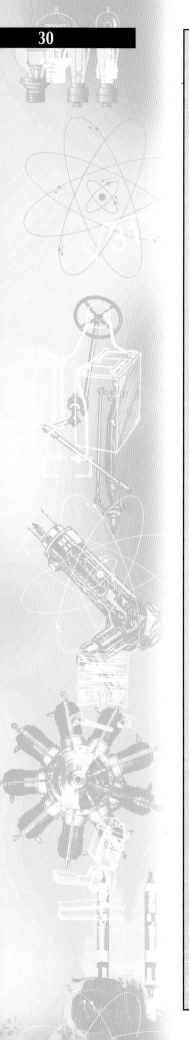

LIGHT HISTORY

300 BC Ancient Greeks such as Euclid discussed the nature of light and how it reflects and refracts.

1010–15 Arab scientist Alhazen described reflection and refraction, and produced early lenses and specially curved parabolic mirrors.

1020 Alhazen said that eyes see by taking in, not sending out, light.

1590 Zacharias Janssen invented the compound microscope, which uses two or more lenses.

1607–08 Hans Lippershey made a refracting telescope.

1609 Galileo Galilei made an improved telescope to study the Moon, planets, and stars.

1621 Willebrord Snell devised the law of refraction known as 'Snell's Law'.

1665 Isaac Newton showed that white light was a mixture of all the colours of light.

1668 Newton invented the reflecting telescope, which uses curved mirrors as well as lenses.

1675–76 Ole Römer made the first reasonably accurate measurements of the speed of light.

1690 Christiaan Huygens argued that light is in the form of waves.

1704 Newton's book *Opticks* said that light is particles, not waves.

1830s William Fox Talbot developed photography as used today. A chemically coated film is exposed to light to produce a 'negative', which can then be used to make many 'positive' prints.

1865 James Clerk Maxwell showed that light is a form of combined electricity and magnetism, called electromagnetic energy.

1880 Electric light bulbs went into commercial production.

1895 Auguste and Louis Lumière showed their early cinema films.

1900 Max Plank suggested that light energy occurred in particles or 'packets', called quanta.

1905 Albert Einstein wrote about the photoelectric effect and how light energy exists in units, quanta.

1926 Gilbert Lewis invented the term 'photon' for a packet or quantum of light energy. Today it's agreed that light can exist as either waves or particles (photons), called the 'wave-particle duality of light'.

GLOSSARY

Concave Dished inwards. A concave mirror curves away from the viewer like the inside of a bowl. A concave lens is thinner in the middle than around the edges.

Convex Bulging outwards. A convex mirror curves towards the viewer like the outside of a bowl. A convex lens is thicker in the middle than around the edges.

Eyepiece lens The lens of a camera, telescope, microscope, or pair of binoculars, which the eye looks through.

Gnomon The upright part of a sundial, which casts the shadow.

Laser light A special form of light where the waves are all the same length, in step, and parallel to each other.

Objective lens The lens of a camera, telescope, microscope, or pair of binoculars, which takes in light from the surroundings.

Pigments Substances that soak up some waves of light but reflect others, to give strong colours used in paints, dyes, inks, and stains.

Primary colours Three main colours which can combine to form all other colours. When light is added, like in a television, they are red, green, and blue. When light is subtracted, like in paint pigments, they are yellow, magenta, and cyan.

Reflection When light bounces back off an object or substance, rather than being absorbed (soaked up).

Refraction When light bends or alters its angle, as it passes from one transparent substance to another.

Retina The light-detecting layer inside the eyeball.

Speed of light The speed at which light travels. It is about 300,000 kilometres per second. It is the highest speed that anything in the universe can travel at.

Transparent Clear or see-through, allowing light to pass through.

Visible spectrum The range of colours of light, due to light having different wavelengths. The colours vary from red, which has the longest wavelength, to violet, which has the shortest wavelength.

INDEX